EMBRACING CHANGE - OVERCOMING THE FEAR AND LEARNING TO LOVE IT

Book 1 in the 21st-Century Spirituality - Ancient Wisdom, Modern Practice Series

WAYNE BEITH

Copyright © 2019 by Wayne Beith

All rights reserved.

No part of this book may be reproduced in any form or by any electronic or mechanical means, including information storage and retrieval systems, without written permission from the author, except for the use of brief quotations in a book review.

CONTENTS

Contact	v
1. Preface	1
2. Introduction	5
3. Why is Change an Issue?	7
4. Active Change	11
5. Cultivating Self-Awareness	13
6. A Path of Change	17
7. Moving Forward	21
8. Hanging On	23
9. New Ideas	27
10. Dissatisfaction	33
11. Accepting Responsibility	37
12. Desire and Decision	41
13. Research	43
14. Action	47
15. The Power of Habit	51
16. Evaluation and Learning	53
17. Repetition	57
18. Dealing with Resistance	59
19. Expect Pushback	63
20. Lifelong Growth	67
21. The Value of Failure	69
22. Sharing the Journey	73
23. Mobility	77
24. Conclusions	81
25. Note	83
26. About Wayne	85

CONTACT

Wayne welcomes contact from his readers. You can contact Wayne through his website or Facebook Page.
   www.waynebeith.com
   www.facebook.com/waynebeithauthor

1

PREFACE

This is a short, to the point book that introduces the 21st Century Spirituality – Ancient Wisdom, Modern Practice series of books and gives you some specific techniques for handling growth and change in your life.

The title of this series, _21st Century Spirituality – Ancient Wisdom, Modern Practice_, sums everything up. The world of spiritual development, the esoteric or the occult (call it what you will) is an old one, or at least one with old roots that reach back right to the earliest days of human existence (and maybe earlier). Yet it is not a static one, because change and the possibility of amazing new developments are part of all human knowledge.

This is a series of books aimed at one thing: supporting you in your personal quest for growth and change, healing, finding yourself, casting off the identity imposed on you by society, family or yourself through fear, and becoming a powerful, integrated and independent person who is following a path you have chosen for yourself.

We can never know all knowledge at any point in time. It is only human arrogance to assume that what we know is all there is to know or that there is only one truth. But assuming that no one actually has it all together offers us hope of improvement, change and the possibility of making a real contribution to the world.

This series of books sets out to explore old worlds and new. We will go on a journey together, jumping between the past, present and future. My emphasis is on practical advice that you can immediately apply in your own life. But I will also be including the theory that you will need to really understand what is going on so that you can make both the theory and practice your own.

In places we will need to deal with difficult topics, and I will try to take you through these in as gentle a way as possible. In still others we will have to deal with uncertainty. There I will present you with all the possible explanations and options (at least that I know of) and leave it to you to determine your personal truth. Lastly you should be prepared to be confronted. I do not pull punches and so I will sometimes be quite blunt and direct about things that I believe will not serve you well.

I've been through this very path of growth and discovery that you are on, and in fact I still am, because it is a lifelong process for all of us. I've made mistakes, gone down paths that later I decided were not right for me, had wonderful experiences, met amazing people and stretched myself till I thought I would snap. In this I've had the support of friends and family, and two strong, powerful women who have been my wives. The first is now in spirit. The second came into my life later and is very much at my side on this path now. And my daughter has now joined now me as well. But there have also been times when I've been on this path by myself, seemingly alone and unsupported. At those times, as now, books like this have helped and guided, and indeed been a friend to me in those dark nights of the soul that we all experience. I hope that in some small way, through these books, and my other teachings, that I can help to support you on your journey, and maybe shine some light to illuminate your way.

❧ 2 ❧

INTRODUCTION

Change is usually confronting. Most of us are creatures of habit, and we seek ways to make our lives as stable as possible. Yes, stability is important, but it is also an illusion. Life is a dynamic process and inherent to that dynamism is change. Learning to deal with change, to control it and our reaction to it, is one of the greatest gifts we can give ourselves.

At the time of writing this I am 59 years old. As I reflect back over my life, so far, there has been massive change, both personally, in the professions I have worked in and in the world in general. I've been divorced and widowed, and am now in my third marriage where we've just celebrated our 20th wedding anniversary. I've changed careers multiple times, from systems programmer to academic, then to journalist and magazine editor, education consultant and back into higher education in various roles. I've established and run multiple businesses. I've done lots of technology consulting. I've switched academic discipline, from almost 20 years in computer science to now almost 20 years in the creative arts. I was born into the cold war, fully expecting a nuclear war with the Soviet Union. Then that collapsed. The new problem became terrorism. Now Russia is an issue again, and China is a looming one. I've gone from a world with phone boxes to very powerful computers in your pocket that have replaced the household phone, camera and much more. I've gone from snail mail to email, Facebook and much more.

The above is all the outward stuff. Of course I've changed massively internally. I've gone from cripplingly shy to much more outward going. My spiritual ideas have evolved massively, as has my understanding of science and technology. My taste in houses has gone from English cottage to brutalist modern. I've gone from hating kids to being a doting father. I've become a mentor to many younger academics.

In all this change, some has been forced upon me, some I've initiated myself while bumbling through life and some has been well planned and prepared for. Change happens no matter what. Given that change will happen, whether you want it or not, there are some things we can do to handle it better. Firstly, we can develop a more flexible and dynamic outlook. Secondly, we can actively introduce change into our lives constantly. And thirdly, we can be on the lookout for the unexpected opportunity. This book is about helping you to do all of this.

Many of the chapters have an exercise at the end. It would be useful if you did these exercises in a notebook or journal so that you have them all in one place.

❧ 3 ❧
WHY IS CHANGE AN ISSUE?

Why is change such a big deal for many of us? To be truthful, it is all about fear. Most of us are hugely driven by fear. Fear of death. Fear of being alone. Fear of not having enough money. Fear of rape. Fear of losing our jobs. Fear of not being liked or loved. Fear of the unknown. Fear of the known. Fear of being wrong. Even fear of being right. We are all bundles of fear, even the least fearful of us.

The advertising industry makes good use of this knowledge of the place of fear in our lives. Ads play to our fears of getting old, being unattractive, having body odour, not being successful, having financial insecurity, not having the latest and greatest gadgets. And so on. Look at any ad and deep down, underneath the need that the ad is claiming to satisfy lies at least one fear.

Fear is a very important aspect of our minds. Without fear to drive awareness we can put ourselves in unnecessary danger. Fear is extremely important for survival. Fear is useful, which is why we teach it to our children so they understand about the dangers of hot objects, traffic and strangers. Fear, when appropriate, helps to keep us alive and functioning. Fear can also, when inappropriate or overblown, hold us back. Fear can paralyse you. Fear can stop you taking opportunities, from growing and developing, from discovering new things.

Life is about achieving a balance between fear and boldness. Without boldness our ancestors would never have come down out of the trees onto the scary plains filled with carnivores, never have learned to tame fire for our own uses and never have expanded into new territory. But without fear they would never have lived long enough to reproduce. So this balance is critical.

So why are we talking about fear and boldness when the issue is change? For the simple reason that change immediately confronts us with this duality: fear and boldness. Change implies a movement from what we know, understand and are familiar with to something or somewhere new and unfamiliar. The unfamiliar is scary.

There is the concept of a comfort zone that you may already be familiar with. Everything we already know, places, people, ideas, form our comfort zone. Outside the comfort zone is new territory. Growth, learning and development only happens when you are outside your comfort zone. A small distance outside of our comfort zone it is not very scary. This is where we are when we are learning new ideas within an already familiar zone. This is the area of slow, incremental growth. Most people can do this fine, though sometimes with a little resistance. The further you go outside your comfort zone the greater the potential benefits because we are dealing with big changes, big opportunities for growth. But the fear goes up the further from your comfort zone you are. So there is a need to be more bold if you are going to stay there and reap the potential benefits.

Timid people never go far from their comfort zone if they

can control it, and move quickly back to the boundaries of their comfort zone, or even well within it, if life circumstances suddenly drag them away. Say we have a friend like this. They may have a partner who is not good for them, perhaps is over-controlling or puts them down all the time. We can see that: our friend unfortunately doesn't. Their partner eventually gets sick of them and leaves one day. We console our friend, point out they are better off without the partner and encourage them to find someone better. But they probably never really take on board that there was a problem with the old partner. One day, probably pretty quickly, they turn up with a new partner who is just like the old one, maybe even worst. We are shocked. But we shouldn't be. Our friend, having been thrown way out of their comfort zone by the first partner leaving them, has jumped straight back in by finding a new partner that they are comfortable with and whose flaws they see as strengths. I have seen this pattern over and over again with clients who have come to me for spiritual counselling or for Tarot readings.

Extremely bold people, on the other hand, love the excitement of being out of their comfort zone. They are high risk takers. They may be addicted to the adrenaline rush triggered by physical danger. Such people may never stick with anything long enough to get the real benefits they could. They change hobbies frequently, jobs almost as often and even partners. They may cheat on their partners for the thrill of the new. They duck out of relationships just before they have a chance to settle into something great.

The trick, and in many ways what this book is about, is achieving a good balance between reasonable fear and reasonable boldness. Let's get going on this journey.

❈ 4 ❈
ACTIVE CHANGE

One of the key ingredients in finding a happy balance between fear and boldness is taking active control of change in our lives. Change is going to happen no matter what we do. But a strange thing happens when we take control: there is less random change and more of the change we want. While I have my theory as to why this is the case, I do not know it for a fact. My theory is that when you provide a conduit for change in your life, the universe doesn't need to impose as much on you randomly. Even some of the major religions stress the need for you to take action yourself. In Christianity there is the concept of "the Lord helps those who help themselves". In spiritual circles there is the idea that you must take action in the physical world so that whatever you are working on spiritually has a path to manifest in your life. It has certainly been my experience that when I am focused on a path of change and development the universe seems to throw less of the "shit" at me. It may be that there is only room for so much change at any given time in a person's life. If I'm busy creating change maybe there is less room for the random stuff. I don't know, but I do know that it works somehow.

How do we set about introducing controlled change into our lives? Well, it starts with having some goal or destination in mind and having at least some objective awareness of your present life circumstance and of yourself. Awareness is critically important. We need the ability of objectively evaluate and reflect on our current life circumstance.

Only when we can objectively evaluate a situation can we be sure that we are not fooling ourselves and are seeing it the way it really is. This is hard. Really hard. For some of us it really benefits to seek the advice of someone else, a friend or someone really objective and detached, like a therapist or counsellor. You'll hear this many times in this book because it is so important. We are often too close to a situation and too invested in it to see things objectively.

5

CULTIVATING SELF-AWARENESS

The rest of this book focuses on ways to build, handle and embrace change, through self-awareness. This focus on self-awareness is spread through the topics covered in the book. But let's first just have a deeper look at self-awareness so you have a framework to work with.

Another expression for self-awareness is internal honesty.

The self-aware are brutally honest with themselves. This can be tough because for most of us it will be novel. We lie to ourselves all the time. About big things and small. The little voice in our head whispers to us, deludes us.

We don't do this to ourselves because we are bad. We do this because we are full of contradictory desires – we want to achieve great things but we also want to lie around on the couch and just watch TV. We want that new job but we are also scared of the responsibility that will come with it. We want to lose weight but we love the taste of sweet things. And so it goes. To make progress you need to understand your competing desires and bring them out into the open.

Self awareness is not about judging ourselves. It is not

about blame or self-flagellation. Generally people do the best they can at any given time. There are exceptions, but broadly speaking, at any given time in your life, with whatever knowledge and self awareness you have, you do the best you are capable of at that point. The issue is not that you are inadequate to the task. What we are trying to do is lift our game, to increase our knowledge, both internal (self awareness) and external, so that the game we are playing in life continues to improve and allows us better to achieve what we want to achieve.

Self awareness is also about understanding our thoughts and our emotions, and making them conscious so we can see what is going on inside us. Too many of our strongest thoughts and emotions have rarely seen the light of day, as it were, been exposed to our conscious and critical evaluation. They hide behind habits.

Habitual behaviour is a defence for the thoughts and emotions that really rule us. Under pressure we slide back into habit. Our habits arose to deal with some situation or circumstance, and they made sense at the time. However, over time, they have become ingrained and get relied on even when they no longer serve us well. Stopping and having a cup of tea and a biscuit can be very appropriate, occasionally. However, when it becomes your automatic response to any challenge, stress or distress in your life it has become a habitual response that may not work well with your other goals of losing weight and being more productive, for example.

Self awareness is bringing into your conscious mind a full understanding of everything that is going on with you, your emotions and thoughts, why you are doing what you are, your real hopes and also fears, to allow yourself to make better, informed choices about your behaviour.

Exercise

Get yourself a nice, blank journal and use it for the exercises that follow in this book, those in other books you may read, notes for courses or workshops you attend and thoughts that come to you over time. Also journal in it. A journal is a wonderful way to keep track of the slow and gradual changes that can happen to you. They remove the burden of having to remember things and there is something very powerful and magical about writing things down. Words have power. Some people prefer to do this on a computer than on paper. For many people the act of hand writing on paper is important. There is a grounding aspect to this, of making things manifest in the physical world, that many people will not feel if they journal or diary on a computer. Others are so well entrenched in the computer world though that they can experience the same grounding effects with a computer journal. This is yet another aspect where knowing yourself is important.

To start on this path of change, begin to write things down, how you feel in situations, what thoughts are popping into your head, what actions you take. Doing this may not come naturally at first. Some of us are more natural diarists, other less so. But persistence is a key characteristic of people who are in control of their lives, so you might as well start cultivating it now. It does not matter how much you write. Just start. Do it daily. At lease once a day allocate a small amount of time to journal what has happened today, how you reacted, etc. Start small. Let it build.

❦ 6 ❦
A PATH OF CHANGE

A path of growth and personal change is not one that can be clearly mapped out in advance. By its very nature, as you make changes to yourself, change your ideas and thinking patterns, cast off old habits and heal old wounds, the path forward will constantly change. Possibilities that you were never aware of suddenly become apparent to you and draw you away from where you thought you were going. Just know that this is all normal and to be expected. It has happened to me and I see it happening to those I am, in some way, involved with helping or guiding.

I went through a period of largely ignoring my spiritual side. This lasted about eight years. I had set off on a path of rational, scientific development. At the time I believed this would serve me well. I didn't realise it at the time, but shutting down the spiritual side also shut down much of my creativity. Years later, when I started actively working on my creativity, it also allowed the spiritual back into my life. I found that the creative side of me and the spiritual both woke up and a huge burst of new ideas and possibilities opened up for me in my life. Since then I have realised that

I've always found the spiritual and creative very interlinked in my life, and when I've been stuck or reached a plateau in one, some work in the other has often been the key to unlocking new progress and overcoming the blocks.

So the path you are on will be one with lots of change and uncertainty. In the beginning that can seem scary. I know I have felt that way at times. There seems to be a security in knowing that you are following a plan. Yet life is actually not one that you can tightly map out. Life will throw you surprise events, some seemingly good, some that feel bad at the time. But let me assure you that, over time, this very uncertainty and fluidity will come to be one of the things you embrace and love, as I now do. The thing about uncertainty is that it is also full of potential and opportunity. If everything is mapped out, planned and determined, then there is no room in your life for the wonderful surprise, the amazing opportunity or for you to create these for yourselves, which is very much what this series of books is about – helping you create opportunities for yourself.

My wife, Adriana, who is my second wife who has shared a path of spiritual development and growth with me, and my third wife in this lifetime, is a great example of the wonders that can happen when you open up to new opportunities. We could have met anytime over about an eight year period. In that time we must have driven past each other, walked past each other or perhaps even waited in the same shop at the same time to be served hundreds of times. But both of us were on a path of change and development that meant that, had we met earlier, it would have amounted to little more than a meeting with a new person who then passes out of your life. But at the point were we did meet, and a very interesting story that is, we had both created changes without ourselves that made it 'the right time'.

We can't always know what the outcome of working on

ourselves will be, but we can be sure that opportunities in life that could be there will never present themselves if we do not work on ourselves to be ready when they do.

For those who need a sense of security in their lives, over time and if you take on the lessons in this book, you will find that the security comes from finding your true self and expressing that in your life. The ways you express that can change through your life. The people you express that with can and will change through your life. The circumstances of your life will change. But through all the change you will be yourself, true to your passions and interests, principles and ways of conducting yourself. And that is the real path to enlightenment.

Exercise

Take your journal and document this process.

Think of a time in your life when you thought your path was all mapped out until something happened to change this. Write down your original plan and then what event or circumstance changed this. Write down the new direction your life took after the change. If this is an old event, you may now have a positive perspective on the event. If recent, you might not yet and you could be finding your life still unsettled or even seemingly ruined by it. Write it as you feel it.

Now, if you are able to, do the following. If not yet ready to, leave some pages empty in the journal so you can come back and do this later in your reading of this book. Think about the original path you had mapped out. Was it really serving you well? Were you really being the true you or perhaps you were being what you thought someone else wanted you to be? What were the positives but also what were the negatives of that path for you? Was the trigger event for the change caused by you or from outside? How did you feel and react at the time? Over time, how did the reaction and feelings about the change modify and develop? Looking back now, how do you feel?

Even if you are able to write quite a bit about this, leave some space afterwards so you can come back and reflect on this further as you work through this book, and afterwards.

❦ 7 ❦

MOVING FORWARD

There are many dimensions to producing personal change and development. In the chapters that follow we'll explore them so that you understand just what is involved.

There are a great many dimensions to growth and development. I would encourage you to take as broad an interest and approach as possible, mixing and matching your points of focus. A varied and diverse attitude and approach will help you avoid the possibilities of getting stuck. For example, being quite academic, it is very easy for me to get stuck in research - I learn a lot intellectually, but with a failure to apply it in practice I sometimes fail to get the full benefit of what I've learned. This is something that I know I have to watch out for. So, for me, I need to mix up research, from very diverse sources, with experiential activities, like workshops and courses, and with my own activities and actions. I have to mix things up.

If we always stay in a nice, narrow little world where we are not exposed to new ideas, ways of doing things or new ways of thinking, then it can become very easy to be satisfied with the status quo. We know nothing else, think this is all there is and so we are satisfied.

This comfortable narrowness was very easy to maintain in previous times, when the entire scope of our lives might have been limited to the village in which we were born.

In the modern world of the Internet, television and radio, books and magazines on every topic, and workplaces and schools where we will likely rub up against people of very different backgrounds, this is getting harder and harder to maintain. We are exposed to new ideas, often challenging ones, all the time and if we want to exclude them we must work harder and harder to block them out.

8
HANGING ON

Since change is uncomfortable, and often more uncomfortable than an existing situation might seem because of familiarity, I see many people working extremely hard to stand still.

We've all done it ourselves and seen others do it too. Someone in an abusive relationship will pretend really hard that it is not, and often they will in fact push that abusive relationship outwards so that it affects other people too. Someone in a high stress, highly abusive job will come home from work and take it out on their wife, husband, the kids or the dog. Kids who are bullied at home will often become the school bully.

Avoiding change is tough. In fact the more imperative the change is, the harder you have to work to avoid it. The Dalai Lama said that all suffering is caused by attachment, and this is so true. Sometimes what we are attached to is actually bad for us.

All situations, and that includes relationships, have a "use by date". Failure to recognise this is the cause of most of our suffering, The harder we try to hang onto something that it is time to release, the more pain we suffer, both in hanging onto it and in the almost inevitable process that will eventually force the release. I have seen this time and time again. And I've done it myself. There was a time with my first girlfriend when the relationship could easily and fairly painlessly have ended for both of us. However, out of my own feelings of inadequacy and total lack of confidence with girls, I kept it going even though deep down I knew it wasn't right. Fear of the unknown kept me there. When I eventually ended the relationship it caused far more pain for her (and everyone) than if I had acted earlier, and I feel very sad about that. She was a lovely person and deserved to be happy, as we all do. Just in the end we were not the right people to make each other happy. There was a time when the relationship was 'right'. But then it wasn't and holding on out of fear just made it worse.

It is easier to see it for others than it is to see it for ourselves. I've seen this with friends and family. I've also seen it with clients who have come to me for Tarot readings over many years. I've seen someone hang onto a bad relationship for so long that eventually, when it was so obvious that it had to end, that they killed themselves rather than face the change. I've seen people hold onto a friendship so desperately past its use by date that, when eventually it ended, it caused far more pain for all those involved than it would have when it was first clear that it needed to end. And I've seen many people have an abusive relationship end and then go out and start a new relationship with exactly the same sort of person rather than run the risk of trying something new.

People crave stability in the false belief that stability means safety and comfort. Now yes, you can have a stable relationship that it good for you. Some people have one great relationship almost their whole life. But so many people don't. There is a deep seated belief in people that what you know is better than the unknown. Sometimes this is true, but often it is not. Even a good relationship can get even better. Even a great job could be more rewarding. Hanging on denies the possibility of improvement.

Please understand that I am also not saying that you should skip out of relationships as soon as they get tough. I'm not. All relationships have highs and lows. All relationships need work. Good relationships change without breaking. Bad relationships or relationships that have exceeded their use by date cannot successfully handle change. Change is a critical part of good relationships. Good relationships evolve over time, get keeping and new dimensions of the relationship are discovered. You have to put effort into relationships, but the work must come from both parties. When you find yourself as the one who is doing all the heavy lifting, then something must be done.

While in the above I have concentrated on relationships, the same applies in other aspects of your life. Work, interests, hobbies, sports, studies and more.

Learning not to hang on is important. So how do we learn to let go?

❧ 9 ❧
NEW IDEAS

New ideas lead to the next ingredient in the process of change.

So what this means in practice is that you should, to the degree that you can deal with at the time, expose yourself to as wide a range of ideas, thinking and experience that you can. It is also good to be open to other people doing this for you. I've generally found that the women in my life are often the very ones who point me in a direction that turns out to be very powerful and transformative for me. I don't know whether it is because they see different things in me than I do, or they themselves are open to a different range of things than I, but the number of times that a woman in my life has, in one way or another, drawn me to exactly the right thing at the right time has persuaded me to pay attention. So if my wife or daughter suggest we go do a course, for instance, my answer these days is always an enthusiastic yes.

This quest for new information and new ideas can be found everywhere. Just because you have a good marriage, for example, doesn't mean that you can't learn something good from books on relationships, or a film. Just because you have a great job does not mean that you can't learn something new from a conversation with a friend, work colleague or a magazine article. Good things can always get better.

The great thing today is that you can expose yourself to a huge range of ideas and experience without spending any or much money. The Internet provides immediate access to a mass of material in written, audio and video formats. Most of us have more channels of TV than we can possibly watch. Try something new. YouTube and Vimeo are amazing resources, including TED talks. Bookshops, whether online or physical, can cover all topics, libraries have great collections and there is lots of good information to be found in magazines. Most areas have community living and learning centres, or community colleges or such where courses can be taken on a wide range of topics at minimal cost. And many more courses are running in any given area, run by individuals. You just have to find them.

We all learn and absorb information differently. So while I can learn well from a book, my wife needs a face to face workshop. My daughter learns well from YouTube videos. I listen to podcasts that auto download to my phone during the drive to and from work, on topics that I am currently focused on, and also a selection that covers broad topics that I might never think to examine.

It is also good to cultivate a wide range of acquaintances and friends. This is an area that some of us can find difficult. You have probably heard people described as extroverts and introverts. What is less widely known is that everyone naturally falls somewhere on a spectrum between extroversion and introversion. Further few people really understand exactly what is meant by these terms. An extrovert is someone who is energised by interacting with other people. They gain energy through interaction. An introvert, on the other hand, is someone who loses energy when interacting with other people. Introverts can find it very tiring to be around others, particularly if the interaction is intense or with lots of people at the same time. Now there is a strong spiritual aspect to this, which is covered int he next book in this series, so we will leave that to there. But here let's concentrate on the physical and psychological.

In an extreme form, an extrovert is someone who does not like being alone, dislikes quiet and comes truly alive when they are 'working' a large room of people. The 'more the merrier' could be their motto in life. Likewise, an extreme introvert is someone who loves being alone, loves quiet and hates interacting with lots of people.

Few people are at the extremes and most of us mix characteristics of both introversion and extroversion. So while I am an introvert and totally hate going to a party or event where I know few or no people, I can be extremely extroverted with groups of people I know well, who I feel comfortable with and who I know are not threatening to me. I am also extremely extroverted when I teach, being very comfortable in the lecture theatre or a workshop teaching. But I need to balance periods of extroversion, which do drain my physical energy if I am not careful, with periods of solitude or quiet time with just a few close people, life my wife and daughter. My wife, Adriana, is the opposite and I've never seen anyone enjoy 'working a room' at a gallery opening or such as much as she does. At the end of the evening she will have spoken to everyone and be buzzing with energy. However, she also likes her 'down time' with just myself and/or our daughter, or a few close friends. So how does this work in a relationships? Actually amazingly well. She pulls me out of my shell and I pull her into smaller, deeper conversations. We also don't try to do everything together. She has her friends, I have mine, and we have many in common. We try to mix activities so that we both get our needs met.

In your quest for new ideas and information you would be wise to seek diversity. While you want friends that share similar interests and ideas, you also want friends who will challenge you. While you want to read information you can relate to, you also need to be exposed to ideas that push your boundaries. Same with your partner in life. Otherwise you can't grow. There is a huge danger in the present media environment. While we have always been able to choose the media we consumed to some degree, for example by reading a left-oriented or right-oriented newspaper, the degree of polarisation in the media has become extreme. There are now clearly left and right wing oriented not just cable TV channels, but whole blocks of related cable channels. The same with radio stations, blogs, podcasts, magazines and more. Same with religious TV and stations, newspapers, and so on. It is quite possible today to consume a huge amount of media that never presents you with a conflicting or different point of view. While many people seem to consider this great, as shown by the rise in popularity of such media, I consider it a true disaster. In producing real and lasting change in our lives our current ideas need to be challenged. Big time. We need to confront very difficult ideas. It doesn't mean we need to necessarily accept them, but we do need to be exposed to them. Would your sex life benefit from watching porn? Would your business be more emotionally rewarding if you understood the lives of poor people better? Would you be a better Christian if you understood something of the life of the Buddha? Would you be a better student if you understood ways of approaching study that your school never showed you? Would you be more creative if you learned how to meditate? Would you be wealthier if you did not need the short-term emotional satisfaction of retail therapy? Would you be happier if you could better accept all the aspects of who you are? Frankly you will never know the answer to any of these or a billion other questions unless you at least explore them to some degree.

Don't get stuck in a rut at where you look for new ideas and inspiration. Try everywhere.

My advice to you is, whatever your preferred way or ways of learning and exploring new ideas and concepts, put in place a program of diverse sources of information. Start small and build. But if you at all can, add in at least one source that has a completely opposite perspective to your own. I do this all the time. When I'm really working on my spiritual growth I'll go read some atheist writing. When I was working on positive contact with the spirit world I went and read some satanist books. I didn't end up as either an atheist or a satanist, but they helped me work out my own thinking and what was right for me. While I am generally slightly left of centre politically, I also read the financial papers every so often to better understand the right-wing viewpoint and to push my own thinking. While I am totally comfortable with technology I also read the writings of people who are struggling with and apprehensive about technology to test whether I have become too comfortable with technology and thus blind to potential issues. Likewise, while I am not religious at all, I have friends who gain great comfort from their Christian, Jewish, Hindu and Muslim beliefs. Conversations with them are always interesting and I learn something every time.

The real value in new information is that it shows us alternatives. This recognition of alternatives may lead us to the next stage, dissatisfaction.

Exercise

So what are you going to do to open yourself up to new ideas?

Sit quietly for a few minutes.

Then take pen and paper and write down some ways you can immediately expose yourself to new ideas.

Go back over the list and put a date by which time you will have started doing this activity.

Take the action.

10

DISSATISFACTION

I believe that the initial real trigger for change is usually dissatisfaction, which comes from a feeling of knowing that there are alternatives and that some of these may be better than what we have now.

We may be dissatisfied with some aspect of our lives, ourselves or our relationships. Sometimes this is a minor feeling that 'surely things can be better than this'. Sometimes it is a major anger and fire in us. Whatever intensity it is, for most of us there needs to be some dissatisfaction, because dissatisfaction gives us the energy to change.

It's been my experience that it is usually better if this dissatisfaction arises from within yourself rather than resulting from somebody else pointing it out to you. When others point things out to us, there can be a level and type of resistance greater than if we figure it out for ourselves, even if deep down we know it is true. For those close to you it can be a hard juggling act of just what to do. Often it is easier for someone else to put their finger on an issue in you that you would benefit from addressing. The big question is do you point this out or not, and a second one is how long do you wait in the hope that the person will figure it out for themselves. This can be very tricky territory.

That's why it is helpful to you (and those around you) if you take some regular time to do a bit of self-assessment and then develop an action plan for dealing with what you find. I do this all the time. Sometimes I communicate what I'm going to do to my wife, sometimes not. I usually don't if it is something that I've noticed in myself which I suspect has not impacted on her. One of the reasons I don't communicate everything I work on is that the last thing I would want is for her to feel pressured to act on herself because I'm always working on something myself. All things in relationships are a juggling act. Lest you worry that there is a lot wrong with me (perhaps there is), let me explain that these will usually be a mix of spiritual, personal and business development areas that I am working on. Many are not so much addressing failings as taking pre-emptive action to address areas that I want to move into later, such as making me a better entrepreneur. I do my self-reflection frequently, usually weekly, trying to answer questions like <u>am I on track,</u> <u>have I found out something new about myself that needs some work</u> or even <u>do I need to better integrate this into myself?</u> I also test if I am coming up against boundaries of my present knowledge or understanding, or have I uncovered a deeply buried block in myself that needs work to clear? This can sound exhausting but gets much easier with time and practice. It actually becomes exciting as you get such a sense of progress as you chip away at things. Also many blocks, bad habits and insecurities actually take a lot of energy from you. Working on them can actually give you more energy.

It can also be helpful if you sit down with someone close to you and honestly ask them what they see might be good for you to work on. Now if you are going to ask you can't be angry or upset at what they say. Take it on board, think about it, and then decide whether to act on it or not. I often do this in the context of sharing some of the things I've decided to work on. In this context it is easy to ask my wife or a friend 'have I missed anything' in a way that empowers them to add their perspective.

It can also be helpful to do this exercise with someone who doesn't know you that well, like a therapist or counsellor. Obviously this would be part of a larger program of therapy.

In each area of my life that I am trying to improve in, I try to introduce new information on a regular basis. At different times in my life the list of areas will differ greatly, as different areas obtain greater importance. One of my driving quests, for example, has been to try to integrate the many different things I am interested in. My PhD work, for example, brought together my passions for art, thought and spirituality. I am continuing this combined interest now post-PhD. At the time of writing I am attempting to bring together my passions for electronics, computers, design and light in the form of designing light fixtures for homes and offices. This is one way that works for me of keeping me focused on change and improvement.

Dissatisfaction often stems from having new information, which is why we talked about obtaining a wider exposure to ideas and experience in the previous chapter. Only when we have more information can we see alternatives to where we are now that we might prefer. Sometimes we need new information to identify something within ourselves that no longer serves us, that we might now be ready to let go of and replace with something else.

Exercise

Take up your journal and a pen.

Sit quietly for a few minutes, breathing deeply and slowly.

Now, without thinking too hard, write down the things that you are currently dissatisfied about, both within you and in your life. Do not focus on what you are dissatisfied with in other people. Just you and your life. Leave lots of space between each item. Don't judge what is coming, just write it all down, one item per line.

For now, just go over it and see if you can add anything to it.

Do not fall into the trap of crossing out things that you think are silly, petty or impossible to change. Let them stand for now.

Keep this list for later.

Come back to this list in a few days and see if there is more you can add. Starting this process will get you working on this subconsciously, so things can also pop up in dreams, in which case add them to your list. Starting on this path makes it very useful to have a notebook beside the bed, as it is likely you will need it more and more frequently. Note that, if you sleep with a partner and having a light on would disturb them, a solution can be to have your phone or iPad at the side of the bed as the screen can be turned right down at night and it is then easy to use to take notes without causing disturbance.

❧ II ❦
ACCEPTING RESPONSIBILITY

Most people are still stuck in the mentality of blaming other people for the things they are dissatisfied with. Sometimes we are solely responsible, often there is shared blame with another, and occasionally complete responsibility lies with someone else. But before we can create change in our lives there has to be the acceptance that there is always something that we can do or try to see if it produces change, even if the change we can work towards is only our own response to some situation or event. This is the beginning of accepting appropriate responsibility for our own lives. I say appropriate because when other people are involved they have their share of responsibility too.

In some situations you will have absolutely no responsibility. Someone who has been raped or abused, for example, has no responsibility at all because these are horrendous crimes that are inflicted on someone and there is no cause except the perversions and cruelty of the perpetrator.

Apart from events like rape, however, the proportions of responsibility obviously vary greatly, but once we are an adult we have to be prepared to accept that our own actions, or inactions quite often, have contributed in some degree to most normal situations we face. It is important though not to be overly generous and take on more than our fair share of responsibility. What we are trying to do here is avoid the victim mentality while also not passing all the blame to others. This is a fine path to tread and some people have more difficulty with this than others.

Accepting responsibility for at least some part of a situation that is affecting you is actually very empowering. If we accept our part then we have started on the road to accepting that perhaps we can effect change.

Even in the case of rape and abuse, we can at an appropriate point accept responsibility for how we let that event that was imposed on us continue to affect the rest of our lives. We cannot control the event, and we have no responsibility for it, but we can (at least to some degree) control how it affects us and what we do with it. This is true of other types of events too.

We can choose to be bitter and twisted if a partner cheats on us, angry and untrusting if a friend betrays our trust and gossips about us behind our back or any number of other reactions to events big and small. Or we can choose a reaction that is life-affirming and positive for us, such as setting out to work on our self-confidence so that we can attract a relationship with a suitably honourable and loving person, work on being firmer about boundaries, offering our support to rape counselling centres, working on our healing while refusing to let events harden our hearts to others, and so on. I hope you get the idea here of what I am trying to suggest. We may not have control over other people's actions, but we do have control over our own reactions, at least to some degree and especially over time. And the path that you are on is all about taking control of our own lives and also of our reactions to situations and other people. We are seeking control.

Our attitude to things is hugely important. This is why the same event can destroy one person's life while seemingly empowering another to a life of high achievement.

The issue is that we all have different personalities, as well as different learned responses and coping skills. Someone who has been given poor coping skills due to the bad parenting they received as a child is not to blame for this at all. That is something the parent is responsible for. But once we become adults then failing to identify your growth needs and setting out to improve yourself is your fault. Yup, I said it.

If as an adult we have a problem within ourselves that we know about and do nothing about it, then we are to blame for everything that follows as a consequence. Likewise, if you know something is wrong in your life but you don't know how you are contributing to it, then failing to work on yourself to gain clarity is again your responsibility.

Somebody, and it wasn't Einstein who is normally assigned authorship of this, said, "insanity is doing the same thing over and over and expecting different results". I've also heard it with stupidity substituted for insanity. The problem is that sometimes all that we know is one way to respond to something. Again the key is to accept responsibility for our response. If we accept responsibility then this enables us to then accept that our normal response is not working for us and maybe it is time to try something new. And that might mean learning so that we can find new responses that are more effective.

Accepting some part of the responsibility for an aspect of our lives, allows us to change it. Even if we didn't cause something, we may be able to control our reactions. That's why this is such a critical step. It is an empowering and life-affirming point of view. Or you can blame everyone else and play the victim. Which do you want?

Exercise

Take the list of things that you are dissatisfied with in your life that you did last chapter.

Against each item on your list, write down what about it you think you are responsible for, no matter how small or how indirectly. Or identify how you are responsible now for what impact you have allowed it to have on your life.

When you are done with one, move onto the next one.

❧ 12 ❧

DESIRE AND DECISION

The real driving force for all change is desire. If we do not desire change then it will not happen, except catastrophically. This is why you cannot change someone else. Being in a relationship with the intention of changing the other person is usually doomed to failure for the simple reason that most people do not want to change.

But if we focus on changing ourselves, then everything and everyone in relationship with you must adapt to your change. Yes, that is right. When you change any aspect of a relationship, or yourself in that relationship, it forces a change on others in that relationship.

Whatever the motivation, a desire to change yourself is critical. It must be a genuine, personal desire to change. It can't be imposed on you, others can't push you to do it, no one else can make the decision of change for you.

The most that someone else can do, with all love, is encourage and support you, perhaps putting the right opportunities and information in front of you. But that is it.

The decision that you want to change is, and has to be, yours.

The reason personal desire is so important is that change can be challenging and take time. Without the personal desire you may not have the stamina for the change.

Coming out of the desire should be a decision to take action. That decision is important in creating a determination to follow through, take action and change.

Exercise

Refer to your list of dissatisfactions. Against each, write a desire that you have regarding it. Short and to the point is perfect. Let's consider an example. Say that the dissatisfaction that you have written down is that you sometimes feel stupid and uninteresting. What you now want to write down is a desire that is possible to address through actions that are open to you. So a desire from this could be to become a more interesting person who can converse intelligently on a wide range of topics.

13

RESEARCH

The next step after deciding that you want and need to change some aspect of yourself or your life is a process of gathering information. This is when you explore different ideas and thinking that are relevant to you and your situation.

This can be a brief process or an extended one. One strong piece of advice I would offer here is to not make this a very extended process. Extended research before action is taken is often just another avoidance or denial process, so be careful of this. We'll have more to say about avoidance mechanisms later. You'll be looping back to this stage over and over again anyway, as we will see. So make this stage as short and focused as possible before you move to the next step.

The forms that your information-gathering can take is very personal and up to you. Many will turn to books, and you might actually be reading this because you are at that stage. It may be workshops, watching a documentary, going and talking to someone, doing therapy or healing work of some kind. Whatever works for you. Everyone is different. In my household I would turn to a book first, whereas my wife and daughter are unlikely to do that and instead would go to a workshop or go talk to someone.

There can be some benefit here in not just focusing on information directly relevant to the particular thing that you are dissatisfied with in yourself or your life, or the desire that you are trying to address. Casting a wider net can be useful, as you will see as we go further.

This research stage will, hopefully, expose you to new ideas and new techniques to apply and practice in the next stages. Let me illustrate with an example.

Some 25 years ago I was at a point in my spiritual development where I was stuck. I had been working on improving my intuition and clairvoyance, but had reached a plateau, as often happens in spiritual development. What I needed was something new to push me into a growth phase again. I had played with Tarot but not really engaged with it. My second wife, knowing all this, went and found a Tarot course with a great teacher and presented it to me as something she was going to do, and did I want to maybe do it too. I said no but she went ahead and booked herself in. Close to the start date for the course she told me she was too unwell to do it and I should go. I did. It was great and provided exactly the unlocking I needed. Had my wife done that on purpose? I don't know, but it is quite possible. Now the reason I am mentioning this here is that the course was part of the research for me. I had been researching Tarot myself and making no progress because the only sources I had examined seemed to be suggesting the correct way to use Tarot was to remember the standard meanings of the cards, all 78 of them. This was not working for me and caused a block. The course opened me up to exploring them intuitively and reading the images on the cards rather than relying on memory. This was the key to unlocking a fruitful exploration of Tarot for me and it also pushed my intuition in very new directions.

It is also in the research stage that you can explore whether the solution to a particular problem might best be tackled with a personal development approach or a spiritual development approach. Or, in other words, is the solution likely to be emotional or mental, or is it spiritual?

Remember that you are not looking for all the answers at once. Development is an iterative process, where you keep chipping away at it until the solution is complete. This is actually a good thing, because some changes you may want to make, if viewed in one hit, may seem too huge. Just remember, a long walk is taken one step at a time.

Exercise

Take the list of dissatisfactions and associated desires that you've been working on.

For each area of dissatisfaction or desire, identify some research you can do that may shed light of the topic. Create an action plan for each and set dates. Do not allow too much time for each of these. It is better to do some research, that start on some actions and then cycle back to more research later. This way you are moving to the action stage as quickly as possible, which is very important.

Now start doing the research.

14
ACTION

Taking action is a very important aspect of change. All the theory in the world is great, but it will probably not produce change in your life or within you. Action is required. Your desire to change must take root in the physical world through action. It must be grounded.

A big part of the power is taking action of any degree. It does not have to be massive or complete and you can take it one step at a time. It is the <u>act</u> of taking action that matters. It is a concept that has even sunk into some of the major religions, such as Christianity's idea "the Lord helps those who help themselves".

So since it is a perfectly normal reaction to see big change as daunting, a better idea is to break a big change up into a series of smaller ones, each with a similarly small action required, that you can take one step at a time. This tricks your brain into believing it is as easy as one of the small steps. Which in fact is perfectly true. Change is never just a one off thing, it is in fact a series of small steps that take you progressively from where you are now to where you want to be.

If you have ever done any business planning, or study or

any such thing, you will have been exposed to the planning process. In planning you break a large task into a series of small steps, make sure the order is right, work out what you need for each step and then monitor progress along the way. Personal and spiritual development is the same thing. Let me give you a personal example below.

One of the things I identified I wanted to change about myself was that I wanted to develop my entrepreneurial skills. The original dissatisfaction was that I seemed unable to manifest as much money in my life as I wanted. The desire was to be better with money and have more ways of drawing money into my life. Now that might seem purely business development, but this desire in fact had personal and spiritual dimensions to it, as you will see below. So below you will see the list of steps I identified I needed to work on:

1. Identification of deep-seated blocks around money caused by family history
2. Healing of these blocks
3. Identification of deep-seated blocks around business and businesspeople
4. Healing of these blocks
5. Repeated work on developing a positive attitude to money and business
6. Identification of my real passions in business
7. Development of an action plan
8. Executing that business development plan in a phased and deliberate way
9. Supporting all the above with creative visualisation
10. Working magically to support the above
11. Identification of deep blocks around commitment and determination
12. Working on clearing those blocks through personal development and spiritual means

Items 11 and 12 only came up when I was well on the path, and so were added to the plan. Now in practice these were not all tackled in the sequence laid out above. Rather, some of them overlapped and some of the later ones were begun way back at the beginning, so that when I really got to that stage some groundwork had been done. I hope this gives you an idea for how this works. I am still working through the steps above, and I am constantly refining it as I grow and develop. Some of the things I am working on now I could not see from where I was starting from. So don't be trapped by a plan either. As you work expect things to evolve. Life is, after all, organic, and so should any process in that life be organic.

The action you take can be very small. So if one of the things you are working on is your willingness to stand up for yourself, then an action on that path might be to say no when asked to do something minor. Practising this on something minor that is less likely to create a major confrontation might be a good first action step. The next time around you try something a little tougher, such as saying no to something more substantial, or saying no to someone who you perceive as more demanding or aggressive.

Exercise

Take your list of dissatisfactions that you have been working on.

For each item on the list, on a new page or sheet of paper develop a multi-step action plan. Some will require many steps, some less. This is fine.

Against each first step put a date on which you will do it or achieve it.

Now get to work.

When you complete a step, add a due date to the next item on the list and continue.

15

THE POWER OF HABIT

Most people are very habitual. We do the same things, in the same sequence, over and over again. We eat the same food, go to the same places and hang out with the same people.

Habits can be a problem, but they can also be a tool that we can leverage in producing change in ourselves and in our lives. Habits happen without us consciously thinking about them. That means that if we can make something a habit we won't have the conscious opportunity to sabotage it. At some level this is how affirmations work: we keep voicing a desired belief over and over again until it becomes ingrained and habitual. I say at some level, because there is far more going on with affirmations than just this. But that is a topic for elsewhere.

So how can we leverage habit in producing change in our lives? There are many ways. Here are a few suggestions.

Since the exposure to new ideas is such a core part of driving change, why not harness habit in this regard. Say you subscribe to a weekly newsletter that is delivered to your email on a Friday morning. Why not schedule in your diary a block of time on a Friday afternoon to look at new material? In this you can start with reading the email newsletter and following up anything that appeals to you. Then you can start using this time to read books, view Youtube videos or such. This way you have a guaranteed hour or two a week of doing this. Hopefully you'll be doing more than that, but at least it sets a minimum. In practice once you start to see the benefits of making change you may find that your appetite for new information becomes insatiable and you'll find yourself doing workshops on the weekend, for example, or reading every opportunity you get.

As another example, say the issue you are wanting to work on is fear of new situations. Perhaps you always go out for lunch at work but always go to the same place. Pick one day a week and make that your 'new lunch place' day. So every Wednesday, say, you go to somewhere for lunch you have not been before. In the beginning this will be difficult and you make all sorts of excuses for not doing it, such as not having time to find somewhere new. You just have to push through this, maybe by just going to the next café down the street after your normal place. Find a way to make this work.

Exercise

Take your list of dissatisfactions that you have been working on and your pages of step-by-step actions.

Go through them and try to identify some areas where you might be able to create a habit. Write these down.

Now make a separate list of these habits and start methodically doing them.

❦ 16 ❦

EVALUATION AND LEARNING

After taking action it is important to give this time, and then evaluate any results or reactions to this action, and then learn something from it.

Giving an action time to settle is important. How much time varies greatly depending on the type of actions you took. Actions that are aimed at producing inner change within yourself, need the most time. These include most spiritual work and some personal development work, such as those working on your emotions and thinking processes, or healing trauma. This is because the change needs to take root in your personality or soul. How long to wait is flexible but I'd suggest up to a month initially as reasonable. It might need much more. Other actions may need little time at all, from immediately to a few days.

The evaluation is really a process of answering these questions:

- Did it work?
- Has the change really taken with me?

- In the process did I discover something else that needs to be worked on?

The answers to these guide your next step, which is why this is an important part of the process.

'Did it work?' seems a simple question but may not be. It may be better to answer the alternative question of 'do I feel different and is that how I would expect to feel if it worked' or even 'can I now do what I hoped to be able to do'. If you have constructed your plan of change in small incremental steps this question may be easier to answer. It is perfectly fine if the answer is 'partly'. You also have to be totally honest with yourself. It is also quite possible that the change has not worked yet at all. More time might be required. We often overestimate how much we can change in a short time and underestimate what we can do over a long time. So a change that we think might only take a month may in fact take six months or even two years. Remember that the longer we have had a particular character trait or thought pattern and the more strongly it has been controlling our lives, the longer it can take to change. There are various ways that we can speed this up, and we cover some of these in other books in this series as some require a very different way of thinking about the world. But things still take time.

Has the change really taken with me? could also be asked as 'can I now keep doing this?' or 'will I now always handle it this way?'. We are trying to assess whether we are on the way to lasting change. I say on the way because all change needs practice over a very long time to be able to say it has really taken. If you've been very shy all your life, and you are now 40, then you have 40 years of being shy to overcome, and that won't happen in a week, or a month or even a year. You'll need to be prepared to keep reminding yourself, to do a refresher as needed and perhaps research and take a new action to reinforce the change. Without a change having really taken there is a natural tendency to slip back into the old ways over time. We've all seen this in ourselves in some way. We make a New Year's resolution to stop drinking soft drink, let's say. For a time we don't. The change seems to have worked. But over time old habits reassert themselves and we slip back. Quite frequently this is because we have not thought the change through sufficiently. We may drink soft drinks partly for the taste and energy, but, deep down, there's familiarity because perhaps our mother gave us soft drinks when we were unwell and thus the image of soft drinks is tied up with issues of nurturing, comfort and safety. For a change to actually take we have to overcome those old associations and develop new, positive ones. This is why the evaluation process is so important. If we start to notice some positive change, even a small one, it starts the process of creating new associations.

Discovering something else when you work on an issue is quite common. For example, you may be working on shyness and in the process discover that you are actually being shy as a defence mechanism because something really bad happened to you as a child that has left you with the deep belief that no one can be trusted. To keep working on the shyness without addressing this deeper issue would be pointless, so identifying this is a very valuable, if disturbing, outcome. You would then work out how you want to start addressing the deeper issues, and then start working on that. If you discover something else that needs to be worked on, take a pause. What you need to do at this point is to re-evaluate. Can you effect change by working on the original issue or will what you have discovered undermine your attempts? If it feels to be the latter, then you may need to change your priorities and do some work on the new issue. In the case of the shyness example above, a reasonable approach would be to first work on our trust issues. Here you might try some counselling. A simple approach might also be to try writing down all the times you have trusted someone and they have not betrayed you. This may show you, over time, that in fact only some people have been untrustworthy in your life. It might then be useful to see if they share any common characteristics that are not also shared with those who have not betrayed you. This process could lead you towards a better sense of who can and cannot be trusted. With this knowledge, working on your shyness may now be effective as you have added a new level of awareness.

Don't be put off by the fact that I point out that some change takes a long time to take with you. I am being realistic. Change is a lifelong process and after some time you start to like it. It can be like the so-called 'runner's high' for the flood of endorphins that people who exercise frequently and heavily get. The thing is, if you never work on change, then you are stuck with the same experience of life over and over again. Dissatisfaction and an understanding that things can change and be better has brought you this point. Keep going.

Exercise

Write your evaluations into your notebook where you have been working on your dissatisfactions.

17

REPETITION

Then you need to repeat the above again. And keep doing it.

Change is never usually a single process that has a definite end. This is because, in the process of changing something, you will find yourself in a new position, with a new viewpoint, and from that new viewpoint you will naturally see yourself, your situation and others differently. Out of this comes a desire for further change, especially feeding off the success you have already had.

Many issues we have can be likened to an onion. You peel off one layer and there's another layer underneath. Change is like this. Removing one layer exposes deeper issues. And you can't stop. Deeper issues will cause us to revert or even invent a new higher-level problematic trait or characteristic if the deeper issues are not dealt with. This is one of the big problems in dealing with addictions. Addictions are a surface manifestation of what many call an addictive personality. Addictive personalities are a result of deeper problems, often tied up with self-worth, nurturing, abandonment, abuse or other personality issues.

Change is, in fact, a lifelong thing. It happens to us whether we want it to or not. So we might as well embrace change and attempt to use it to our own ends, to move us closer to where we want to be, accepting that as you go on the journey you just might change your mind about where you want to go. And that is fine.

❧ 18 ❧

DEALING WITH RESISTANCE

The aspects of yourself that you most want and need to change to move forward will probably be the ones that put up the biggest fight to stop you from changing. Even though at one level you have made up your mind to change, at other levels of your very being there will be an equally strong attachment to them. They are familiar and there is comfort in the familiar, even if they also cause you pain. So there will usually be resistance. We all know resistance. It may take the form of that little voice in your head that tells you 'others won't like you if you change' or 'you can't really do this, so why try', or even 'you are not good enough to deserve this'. It may take the form of you getting sick, developing an injury or you go out and spend all that money you were planning to use on that course you wanted to do. We have many ways of sabotaging ourselves. Most people have learned many avoidance strategies to stop themselves from changing.

Part of knowing yourself (it's <u>basic</u> to the spiritual life at any level) is in figuring out your own self-sabotaging strategies and finding ways to control them. Ultimately it all comes down to this: is your desire for change greater than your inner desire to stay the way you are? This is why the dissatisfaction stage is so important in giving you some motivation and strength behind the desire to change.

We are all different in the best way to motivate ourselves and overcome resistance. Generally people fall into one of two camps: reward seekers or punishment avoiders. If you are in the former, you could focus on what the rewards and benefits to you will come from making the change, or you could put in place a real reward structure, such as if I make this change I will reward myself with a trip. If you are in the latter then you need to focus on how the existing situation is hurting you by causing missed opportunities, for example. Or find a way to punish yourself should you not stick with the program.

Avoidance strategies can be very subtle. The need to constantly check email just in case something important comes in from the boss or someone else is a common 21st-century avoidance strategy. I'm too busy, there is no time, there is no money are also common ones. If you use the email one, try closing down your email program except for set times of the day. Limit your Facebook time similarly. If there is no time, try getting up half an hour earlier. And so on.

A degree of stubbornness is also very beneficial.

A support network can also be very helpful here. This could be your partner, a friend, a writer's group or some other support group. For some, finding genuine supporters of your change can be hard, particularly with people who have a self-interest in the old you.

Exercise

In your journal or notebook, write down the negative thoughts about change that come to mind. Spend some time on this.

Once you have a list of negative ideas, go back over them

and reflect on them. If you have insights into them and perhaps can destroy them, then write it down.

Reflect on your self-sabotaging strategies. Document them in your journal.

Now look back over your self-sabotaging strategies and attempt to identify times in your life when you have used them and what they stopped you from doing.

For each of your self-sabotaging strategies, spend some time brainstorming approaches you can take to avoid or control them.

Then take action.

❦ 19 ❦
EXPECT PUSHBACK

People have a relationship with the person you used to be. When you change, others will notice, though perhaps not consciously. And they will have their own opinion about it. They may like your changes or they may not.

The problem for many people is that, when you change, it changes the dynamic of the relationship they have with you and they have to change in response. And if they liked the way things were, you can expect a negative reaction. Sometimes it is because they have fears about change and so seeing you change pushes their own buttons. Or the relationship may have served their interests the way it was and either now you are not cooperating in their game plan or have changed the game completely. The reaction will be strongest with people who seek to control you and manipulate you in some way, especially if the changes are making you stronger and more independent.

In your intimate relationships you can also expect reactions for the same reasons as above. If one of the reasons you are working on change is because of a less than ideal relationship with your partner, you can expect particularly strong pushback from them. They may not know what is going on, but there will likely be a reaction of some kind. Be particularly careful of emotional blackmail at this time.

A good, positive relationship handles change well. It adapts and is flexible to start with. A poor relationship is rigid and handles change badly.

Relationships with parents and siblings can also be problematic when you are working on self development. Parent and sibling relationships can have very long established patterns and little self awareness. They can also include a lot of manipulation and control. So there can be very real resistance to change.

Handling it

Handling pushback in any form can be tough when you are probably feeling vulnerable and somewhat unsure about the changes you are making anyway. The key is to ignore the pushback as much as you possibly can and recognise that if people have a problem with you changing, then that is their problem and not yours. You may need to confront the problem and establish boundaries. Or sometimes ignoring it and just getting on with life works best, leaving them to deal with it. Only you can tell what is appropriate for you in your given circumstances.

Having someone to talk to who is either supportive of the changes you are trying to make, or is a neutral observer, can be really beneficial. They can help you work out what is going on with people's behaviour around you and suggest strategies for dealing with it. You can expect people's behaviour to get really weird at times.

Sometimes it can be helpful to have visible and loud supporters of your change within the group where resistance is strongest. Think of them as a cheerleading team. So if there is resistance in you family but there are one or two supporters, encourage the supports to back your change path with the others.

Expect breakages

You also need to be prepared that some relationships will be stretched beyond breaking point and will come to an end. That happened to me with my first marriage, when I was working on change and my partner was not. I changed, she didn't and suddenly it was very obvious that the relationship was no longer working for either of us. I've also lost friends whenever I've had major changes in my life and when I was in a process of actively working on myself. The key thing is not to hang on. Recognise that relationships can have a use-by date. When it is time for them to end there is usually more pain in trying to hang onto something than there is in recognising it and letting it go. It is also a better affirmation of your own power if you make the decision rather than having it forced on you. Of course sometimes you won't recognise this and will hang on believing it's still a relationship that is right for you. My experience has been that circumstances will conspire to end the relationship anyway, just probably with much more mess than there needed to be. Sometimes we need that, and of course hindsight is a wonderful thing. It can be far less obvious at the time.

One way to think of this is as making space in your life for something or someone new and better to come in. People and things take up space in our lives. I believe that each of us has a personal limit of how many people and how much stuff we can have in our lives. For some it will be small, for others large. But I have found it to be consistent for an individual throughout their life. Some people will naturally have a large friendship circle, others a small one. So there is a very real need to make space if we want something new in our lives. With an active program of change it can be important to surround ourselves with people or things that affirm that change. This means you also have to let go, it is that simple. Remember that saying, "as one door closes, another one opens". We just have to have the guts to open that new door and step through it.

Just do your best and stop kicking yourself afterwards, or blaming others.

Extra information

There are spiritual ways to protect yourself from pushback and to help with how difficult people can become when you are changing. Most of these fall into the category of spiritual protection and I direct you to my book on Spiritual Protection, in this series, for practical information on how to handle this.

Exercise

In your journal or notebook, note where you are experiencing the most pushback.

Consider each of these in turn and see if you can identify what that person or group got out of the old you that they might feel at risk of losing now.

For each decide on a strategy to take.

Write all this down and review it over time. Note in the journal any breakages that occur. See these as a positive thing that makes room in your life for someone or something better.

❧ 20 ❧

LIFELONG GROWTH

Life is change. Without change there is no life. So to resist change is to resist life. It is, in fact, to kill yourself effectively. People who don't change become stuck and negative; they act as a drag on those around them and can easily become a negative force in people's lives. We all know people like that.

You don't want to be that. You want to be alive and vibrant.

Alive and vibrant people are changing and adapting all the time, trying new things, failing, and still going on to try new things again.

The next chapter talks about the value of failure, so for now stop yourself getting trapped into self criticism when something you have tried doesn't work out as planned. That's life.

Life is a continuous process of change, growth and learning. You can change anything, potentially. Of course others may be resisting your change attempts, so things may not necessarily move or go the way you hoped. But that may just mean that you need to try another way. Or it may not be the right time for that change to occur. And if there is one aspect of your life that you cannot change yet, tit can be easier to deal with if there is plenty of change happening in other areas, so concentrate on those.

What matters so much is your frame of mind. If you can become comfortable with the idea of continuing change it liberates you in so many ways. It takes away the fear that an unpleasant situation in permanent. A good situation can get even better. Your wants and desires will change over time, so that what was once a great situation can later seem much less so. Then you work towards change in a new direction. Of course there is also the possibility that a good situation can go bad. But you know what? That can happen anyway and we have all had that experience of something that we were really enjoying going bad for no obvious reason. In other words change is going to happen to you whether you actively participate or not. Now you can either stick your fingers in your ears, hum a song and pretend it's not happening, or you can accept that things change and at least try to control as much of it as you can to produce change in directions that you want.

It can sound tiring, but remember that it takes at least as much energy to stay still as it does to move, usually more. You can sometimes exert so much energy on maintaining a situation that wants to change that it would actually be like a holiday to accept the change and move with it. Of course sometimes this is only really apparent with hindsight.

21

THE VALUE OF FAILURE

We often have a built-in fear of failure, which comes from childhood and silly ideas from school that there is always a right answer. Usually there is no right answer in an absolute sense. Rather, there are many possible answers, some more desirable perhaps, some less so, depending on how and from where you are looking at the situation.

The most successful people fail frequently. But they do not beat themselves up over it. They just recognise that this approach did not work, and so they go on and try something new. Most entrepreneurs will have had a number of businesses fail, sometimes spectacularly, before they hit something that works. Failures didn't stop them, why let them stop you?

The only way to not fail is to never do something hard or new. If you always stay within what you know well you minimise your risk of failure. But then you are not growing. We grow when we are working outside our comfort zones, pushing ourselves. And sometimes when we are pushing boundaries we will fail.

The way to deal with this is to accept that failure is a possibility and that it is not a disaster if it happens. You will learn valuable lessons from the failure that you can apply next time.

The key to making the most of failure is to learn from it. See if you can find out why it didn't work. Sometimes there will be no obvious reason. Often there will. Sometimes there are many reasons why it didn't work. It doesn't mean that trying the same sort of thing in the future still might not work, because circumstances might be different. But it may also mean that there were things you didn't know or hadn't sorted out properly that contributed to the failure. That is gold. Work on those, learn from them and move on to try something else. Be better prepared next time.

Sometimes the worst thing is for the early things you try to all work well. Some people seem to have a charmed early life and things just work for them. This seems ideal but can have a very negative side. Such people fail to develop the resilience that someone who has experienced failure early and has pushed through it will have. This can lead them to having a very low tolerance of failure when it inevitably happens. If this has happened to you then it might be useful to concentrate on the fact that you happened to be lucky with the early work and rejoice that it happened, without falling into an expectation that this will always be the case. Hidden in among all that early success will still have been failures, even if minor. Remember them to remind yourself that life is always a mix of successes and failures, for everyone.

The right attitude to have to failure is that failure is only an indication that you pushed boundaries and it didn't work this time. That's it.

The worst thing you can do is let failure slow you down, or even stop you cold. Momentum and movement are keys in this world that is, in fact, always changing around us. It may look the same, but this is an illusion; in fact it never is. The world around you is changing, so keep mobile yourself.

Failure is as natural as success, and actually essential for it.

And sometimes what we think was a failure only seems that from the limited position that we currently occupy.

Exercise

Think back to a big failure that you had a long time back in your past.

We pick something a good while back in the hope that some of the emotion has gone out of it.

Really deconstruct the failure: what was considered to be lost at the time, what were the immediate consequences, how it made you feel about yourself.

Now think forward in time. Was it really as bad as it seemed at the time? Did something positive come out of it? Did you learn something valuable out of the loss? Was there some unexpected positive follow-on event that could not have happened without the 'failure' creating room in your life?

If you picked an event that you cannot identify anything positive about then it may be still too fresh (even if a long time ago). Pick another, further back in time and perhaps less major and do the exercise again.

Even if you picked something the first time that you can identify positives from, still pick another 'failure' and do the exercise again.

In total, do this exercise for at least five 'failures'.

When you look at all five I hope you can see that some failures actually weren't failures at all when you take a long enough perspective. Some looked like failures but in fact were not as bad as they seemed at the time and some the lessons learned were so valuable that it was worth the price you paid.

You may also find that in the process of doing this you reconsider some of the first failures you did in the exercise.

Sometimes you have to take a step backwards so you can move in a new direction.

22

SHARING THE JOURNEY

So far we have concentrated on you alone. But there is no reason why your path to change needs to be walked alone.

There are many like-minded individuals out there, and some of them you may already know. If you are fortunate, your life partner will be one of them and they will encourage you in your quest, just as you will them. In other cases a partner who can be reasoned with can be encouraged to see your necessity for change. Beyond your partner, you may also find family who are on a similar path. People often do not talk about such things with those close to them for fear of rejection or of upsetting the status quo. Often it just requires someone to have some courage.

If you have a partner who is not interested in change and, in fact, is actively discouraging you, then you have to decide how to deal with this. The easiest path might be to work on your change without telling them. They will, probably subconsciously, feel that something is going on, but at least you may be able to avoid the arguments of open discussion. In other cases it is better to make it known that you are working on change for your own benefit. Their support or not will make no difference and if they really cared they would be supportive; you can leave it to them to deal with it or not. Only you know the dynamics of your relationship. I will say that my view is that no one should allow themselves to be held back by another person, no matter how important they might seem to be in your life. Someone who deserves you in their life should be supportive.

You may also find like-minded people in your friendship circle. Often all it takes is a willingness to talk about your desires and plans. They may have also been uncertain about discussing their desires for change with you.

Outside your friends and family, how do you find people to share the path of change with? The obvious one is through groups and workshops. People participating in groups and doing courses are usually seeking change, so that's a starting point. The key here is to be open and willing to talk to strangers. At least if they are in the same group or course you know that you have at least one thing in common. This might make it easier and can serve as the starting point for conversation.

Shyness and fear of rejection is common. Most people have them to some degree. I know I do. It is sad to say, but in reality the only way to overcome these is to just talk to people anyway. The first one can be hard, the second a little less so. It gets easier the more you do it. Trust me, it really is that easy.

You can also find people on a common or similar path online. Facebook or LinkedIn groups, discussion forums and more allow you to find people with at least some common interest and start building relationships with them. I have made some wonderful friends like this, some that I have never met and others that I've been fortunate enough to meet up with when travelling. Like anywhere, you can also meet unpleasant people online, just as in groups and courses. Do not let them deter you.

The great majority of people that you will meet in groups or courses, face to face or online, will be wonderful people, some of whom you will really click with and with whom you can forge great friendships.

Having at least some like-minded individuals in your life is a huge benefit. You will have people to talk things out with, to support you when you hit a rough patch and to share knowledge from a slightly different life experience perspective.

Over time you will build up a network of people who mutually support each other.

Exercise

Spend the time to find at least one online and one face to face group or course that you can attend or participate in. Practise being open and being willing not only to listen to and help others, but also to be willing to share your own experience and concerns.

Then repeat this again.

You may need to try different groups as you grow and develop, as your ideas change. That's normal. Don't be afraid to leave a group that is no longer working for you. This is not a rejection, just an acknowledgement that you have changed and so your needs may have to. There are plenty out there, just go and find some new ones.

23
MOBILITY

The world is a changeable place. Things change all the time. On the surface it may look the same, but dig deeper and it never is.

In a changing world, where our friends and business associates are concentrating on new things, where there are new undercurrents flowing through life, culture and the economy, where there are new ideas flowing into the world all the time, mobility and flexibility are key assets.

Most of us like stability because we like things to be predictable. This is a deep survival mechanism and the history of our development as a species has been one of using our advantages to gain more and more control over our environment so that we had stability. We farmed so that we weren't dependent on the changing movements of prey animals. We built cities of safety and more stability. And so on.

But stability is a big illusion. It is fake. Yes, things can be stable for a time. But we tend to want to extend that over longer and longer periods of time. And we will expend amazing energy and make amazing compromises to try to maintain it. This is why people stay in bad relationships with abusive partners. It is why people stay in soul-destroying jobs. And on the big scale it is why we continue to do things we know will ultimately destroy the very environment that we depend on to live.

So if stability is an illusion in reality, how do we deal with it? Develop a mobile mentality.

Mobility means that we are not fixed in our thinking or action. We are willing to do things differently, to adapt to change, to drop something that is not working and try something else, anything else. Entrepreneurs talk about the ability to 'pivot' a business. Pivot means to change. Change direction, develop different products, try something new. They use the word pivot because it carries less emotional baggage with it than other words that could be used, like failure, try again, move on, etc.

Pivoting requires flexibility. Flexibility gives you mobility. Mobility lets you react to change early, perhaps gaining huge advantages over others through seeing a change early, before others, and reacting to it positively, embracing it.

You want to do everything you can to cultivate flexibility and mobility in yourself. Trust me, it will come in very handy.

Exercise

Find some quiet time and take out your journal.

On a new page reflect on the times in your life when you have not demonstrated flexibility and mobility. Also reflect on what the consequences were. Write these down. Take as much space and time as you need.

Now on another new page, reflect on times when you have been flexible and demonstrated mobility, and note how it worked out for you. Likewise, take as much time and space as you need.

Now compare the two. Be honest with yourself. In the case of the times you were not flexible, think back and work out just how early you could have seen the warning signs of pending change, how you might have responded to them early and what the outcomes might have been if you had done so.

Now, on a new page, document the areas in your life that feel stuck, or that have become unsatisfactory in some way. For each one, reflect back and identify just how long ago you could have recognised the warning signs. Don't beat yourself up about this. We are always changing. You are changing, so you are no longer the person who did not recognise things when you could have. We are not judging ourselves. We are learning and affirming not to repeat patterns which have not worked for us in the past. Now, for each of the stuck or unsatisfactory areas you have written down that are in your life at present, brainstorm ways that you can pivot, ways that you can demonstrate mobility. Spend as much time on this as you need. If you need to, go look up brainstorming on the Internet and get some ideas on how to proceed. For each create several action steps if this is necessary, or a single step for the simple ones. Assign dates to when you will do then, then start doing them.

REMEMBER:
  No judgement
  You are where you are
  That is all
  Now start moving
  Towards where you want to be

24
CONCLUSIONS

Change is part of life and coming to terms with it, embracing it and making it work for you is one of the greatest gifts you can ever give yourself. Hopefully this book has given you some useful tools to handle change in your life. Now go and practise them.

25
NOTE

The information provided in this book is the author's view and does not constitute advice for your own actions. No responsibility is accepted for any mishaps or damage you may encounter on your spiritual path. Use common sense and do not do anything that you are not completely comfortable with. And thus accept the responsibility for your own actions.

Any resemblance to any person living or dead is purely accidental.

26
ABOUT WAYNE

Wayne grew up in an esoteric family with a long history of spiritual practice in various forms. So Wayne's path has taken him from his ancestral beginnings through a lifelong journey of exploration and growth.

A teacher by nature, Wayne has and does teach many topics within the esoteric, does counselling of people with a spiritual orientation and writes.

Wayne's PhD is in art with a strong spiritual linkage. He has a wife and daughter and lives in Australia.

www.ingramcontent.com/pod-product-compliance
Lightning Source LLC
Chambersburg PA
CBHW030604020526
44112CB00048B/1212